The Un-Chosen Life

My Life A Living Testimony

In this book are _The Seven Keys To Success_ and _How To Study Smart Not Hard._ I have also included other skills the Lord taught me in my walk through this _Un-Chosen Life._

Carmen M. Correa, Ms.C, Ms. Ed.

WESTBOW
PRESS
A DIVISION OF THOMAS NELSON
& ZONDERVAN

Scripture taken from the King James Version of the Bible.

WestBow Press books may be ordered through booksellers or by contacting:

WestBow Press
A Division of Thomas Nelson & Zondervan
1663 Liberty Drive
Bloomington, IN 47403
www.westbowpress.com
1 (866) 928-1240

ISBN: 978-1-4908-7120-2 (sc)
ISBN: 978-1-4908-7121-9 (e)

Library of Congress Control Number: 2015903121

Print information available on the last page.

WestBow Press rev. date: 03/05/2015

Contents

Dedication

I dedicate this book in loving memory of my mother Matilde, who unknowingly, taught me how to be a good wife, a good keeper of my home, and for a short time, a good mother. I love you and miss you.

And to my husband Wilbert, who passed away a week before his birthday. He was the one who inspired me to put this book in your hands. I did not believe that my story was interesting enough to share with others, but he would tell me that my story was inspirational to the spirit of God in everyone who reads it. I miss you so much honey.

Acknowledgement

My Lord and Savior Jesus Christ, who gave me life when I was dead in sin and inspired me to write this book. I want to thank Him for walking with me through all of my experiences that have changed my ways from my own to God's ways of doing things. I thank Him for taking all my pain and leaving just the scars to remind me of His power and love. I thank God so much for His mercy that spared my life so many times. Thank you Father for loving me so much, that He gave His Son to die for me.

I would like to acknowledge my sister in Christ and best friend Gwen Gause. She edited my first draft. She will be surprise to read it now. Love you!

I would like to say thank you to my friend and teacher, Wanda, who took time out of her very busy schedule to edit my final draft.

To my niece Rachel, who spent some time with me and typed for me when I could not do it. I enjoyed that time together. Thank you and I love you.

The Un-Chosen Life

What would our lives be if we had a choice?
The reality of life is that we don't have a choice
Our lives have been predestined
When we know our destiny we can fulfill it with
gladness, knowing it is God's Will.
(Rom 8:29 – 30) (Eph 1:5, 11)

All Scriptures are from the King James Version
Of the Bible unless noted otherwise.

Author Foreword

I LIKE THE SAYING:

"You don't know where I am going,
If you don't know where I have been."

Many of you would say that "everybody's life has a story "and that is true. There are so many stories in this world that there would never be enough paper on which to write them all. Many are stories of sadness and many of horror, some of joyful times and some of miracles like mine. Many people walk around in this world with a story that could set others free from poverty, drugs and/or alcohol. However, they keep it to themselves. The question is; what is our story for? It is for a _TESTIMONY._ I believe we each have a testimony to share, in hopes that it will help someone else. Testimonies set free those who are bound and to encourage those who need to be encouraged. This is my hope for writing this book not just to tell you about me and the hardships and joys of my life. I want to tell you how I came through so that you can go through _successfully._ The key words are "getting through successfully." It is like a test and 99 and ½ will not do. You need to score 100% to pass.

I pray that not only will you come through successfully, but also come into a place where you can feel peace, power, and joy, knowing that "all things work together for the good of those who love the Lord (Rom 8:28)." To be able to love others who have hurt you. To stand on the Word of God even in the midst of our storms is the goal for a Christian. With this knowledge we can walk towards happiness and have the courage to face the future. As I guide you to where I have been, may you find places that are similar to your journeys or sights you have seen. You may encounter a place you have never been to before and are now aware of it. You may be enlightened about an area that was once darkness.

You can learn much from this book. However, there is one thing I truly hope you will understand and that is the devil will try to keep you from knowing the power God will give you when you stand on His Word, who is His Son Jesus Christ. I want to stress one point; that God has CHOSEN all of us to be SAVED. He wants NO ONE TO PARISH and we who know this wonderful news must tell it to the world.

Introduction

This book flows in a time line that takes you back to the womb, where the story begins. It then takes off into an array of incidents that are forever burned into my field of memories. These create a personal character, full of hope for the life that is to come. You will be taken into areas of amazement and fear. You will visit a place through the eyes of a child and then seen from the eyes of an adult. There are miracles that cannot be explained, but God is real and is still in the miracle-working business. The faith that moves mountains can restore the life that once was dead. Events like these encompass this book. Final, you will learn how I came to the realization of my calling and finding the purpose for my *Un-Chosen Life.*

The Bible tells us that, "Many are called, but few are CHOSEN" (Matt 22:14). The question now becomes, what is the difference between the lives of the CALLED and the lives of the CHOSEN? Is there a difference? The answer is an unequivocal "yes." The CALLED can CHOOSE to follow the Lord Jesus' life. The CHOSEN must live out the life that God has CHOSEN for them. The CHOSEN must live their lives according to God's Divine Will. They have no CHOICE. It is *The Un-Chosen Life*

Why do I call it *The Un-Chosen Life!* Well, if the CHOSEN had a CHOICE, would they have CHOSEN the life they have lived or will live? Would they CHOOSE to walk the road that they have walked or must walk (Acts 9:15-16)? This is probably why many are CALLED, yet a few are CHOSEN (John 15:19).

The life of the CHOSEN is not a life of CHANCE, but a life of precision. It's not a path of CHOICE, but a CHOSEN path. A life of accomplishments against all odds is the substance of the life of the CHOSEN. A CHOSEN life is one that must be endured until his/her purpose is fulfilled. CHOSEN people do not have a CHOICE on the paths their lives take. They must fulfill a destiny already planned before they were even formed in their mother's womb. There is no greater desire in the heart of a CHOSEN person than to fulfill his or her destiny. Nothing becomes more important than the fulfillment of the path CHOSEN by God, which becomes <u>THE UN-CHOSEN LIFE.</u>

How would you know if you were CALLED or CHOSEN? God puts such a desire to do WHAT He has put inside of you to do. When you meet a person that has endured so many obstacles and hardships in life, and still fulfills the plan God CHOSE for them, that is a CHOSEN SOUL. How would you know the difference between the CALLED and the CHOSEN? Those who under the same circumstances would quit are the CALLED. The CHOSEN will accomplish his/her destiny against all odds, because it's the wind that propels the sails of the CHOSEN forward. I know the difference between them, because I am CHOSEN (Jer. 1: 5, NIV, Gal. 1: 15, NLT).

The Title of This Book

I first wanted to name this book <u>THE HURDLER.</u> I felt that my life was all about jumping hurdles and, therefore, this book would be a help to those going through the hurdles of life. In our lives we all face hurdles. Hurdles have no respect of persons. The mere fact that we all face hurdles in our lives makes us a global world. Now, the way we deal with hurdles in our lives differentiates us one from another. This was the part that changed the title of this book. As I looked deeper into the hurdles of my life, I came across a difference that set some people aside from others. That was their ability to ENDURE even in adverse situations.

This information enlightened me, and I searched the Scriptures to find those who had been CHOSEN, and I read about their lives. I found scriptures where the Lord talks about the CHOSEN such as in II Chronicles 29:11, "…..for the Lord has CHOSEN you." Haggai 2:23, "I will make you like a signet ring, for I have CHOSEN you." And Matthew 12:18, "Behold, my servant whom I have CHOSEN." After reading such lives of these CHOSEN people, I learned to submit myself to this power within me that kept telling me that I would be great; that there was something about me God liked. The minute I surrendered all to Jesus, my Lord, things in my life took off. Things fell into place like a puzzle, where every piece had its place and I knew where every piece of my life belonged.

There are many other scriptures that specifically point out the chosen by God. This knowledge changed the title of this book from *THE HURDLER to* THE UN-CHOSEN LIFE; now the events that occurred in my life made sense.

I know that if I had had a CHOICE in the way I lived my life, it would have been different. Yet, I know that I would not be who I am today, had I not experienced what I did. As I mentioned earlier, the life of the CHOSEN is not a life of chance, but a life of precision.

Looking back at the events of my life, I see how they meshed with my thoughts, feelings, and reactions to the events of my life today. The question you are probably asking yourself now is, what does this book have to offer you? I have taken the liberty of using the philosophy: "You will not listen to a poor person tell you how to get rich, but you will listen to a rich person tell you how to get rich." In this way, I say by understanding how the events in my life, which are many, served a purpose, you will learn to see how the events in your life serve a purpose. You may even discover what that purpose may be.

Ask yourself the following questions: If someone told you or showed you how to make your life easier, would you listen? If I had never had that experience, would know how another person handled that experience help me if I ever had to walk in that experience? If you answer "yes" to either or both questions, then you need to read on. Many of us walk through life not knowing how to deal with or overcome some situations we encounter. I pray that this book will serve such a purpose.

By hearing about my life experiences and God's interventions, it may convince you to allow God into your life. You may even learn what to do before trouble happens. Someone responded to me, when I asked, "Why me?" That person said, "Someone must go through it to be able to tell others how they can get through." Just like the three men in Daniel 3:21 – 30, Shadrach, Meshack and Abednego, who went through the fire, yet "the fire did not affect their bodies nor the hair of their heads. Nor were their trousers damage, nor had the smell of fire even come upon them."

There is no need for you or anyone who reads this book to go through any situation without knowing how to get through successfully. The secret is getting through successfully. This is the reason why a recovered alcoholic can tell an alcoholic how he or she can overcome.

That person has gone through the suffering and pain with alcoholism. Once that person has overcome the grip of alcoholism, he or she can help others by sharing his or her experience (Testimony). They can help others overcome with less pain and suffering, because they learned the hard way and are willing to share their stories, enabling others to overcome with fewer struggles. People are more likely to listen to someone who, has been there, seen it, and has overcome it successfully and won't go there anymore.

The presentation of my experiences and their outcomes will be as a narrative autobiography. If this book helps you discover God's plan for your life and how to get over the hurdles, even if it is only one hurdle in your life past or present, then this book has served its purpose. Hosea 4: 6 states: "Because of a lack of knowledge my people perish."

Many of us die physically or spiritually, because we don't know any better. If this book saves one life or encourages one person, then the battle has been won.

Some people will turn to alcohol and /or drugs to solve their problems, not knowing that they will in all likelihood create even greater problems for themselves. This is the reality of human nature. Many of us cannot see beyond the hurdles that stand before us. We therefore, accept the situation, coming to the erroneous conclusion that there is no way out. We tell ourselves, "this is the way it is and this is the way it is going to be." We take on the feeling of helplessness. If we could accept the events of our lives as another way to obtain knowledge to help others, then the situation does not control us. Then we can contribute to a positive outcome.

Again, I want to state that we all have hurdles in our lives, but the way we deal with them is what differentiates us one from another. God has a purpose for your life. You are not on this earth by chance. You have been CHOSEN.

Finding Out God Had CHOSEN Me

One morning as I was meditating and praying, I was taken back in time. It seemed like I had lapsed into a trance. I saw my life flash before me. It took me as if back to my mother's womb. I saw my twin sister. From what my mother told me, my sister had died two weeks prior to our birth. Mom was unaware that she was pregnant with twins and conjoined (attached to each other) twins at that. We were attached to one umbilical cord.

We were born in a small hospital that had no ultra sound machines to detect how the baby was doing. In those days midwives usually assisted with the delivery of the baby. The local hospital was used only in cases of emergency. My mother delivered some of her older children at home with the help of a midwife. With us, my mother was having unusual discomfort. Two weeks prior to our birth, my mother felt as if the baby had dropped. When the midwife arrived, she told Mom that the discomfort was just the baby moving into position to be born.

Days passed and Mom continued to feel bad. She just knew that something was definitely wrong when her nails began to turn blue and she could hardly walk. Mom could still feel the baby moving and felt comforted that the baby was still alive. She had no idea whatsoever that the drop she had felt two weeks earlier was my twin sister detaching from me and the umbilical cord we shared. My twin died in the womb. Mother told me that when the doctors removed my twin sister, her skin had begun to deteriorate. However, no one was aware that I, of course, remained attached to the umbilical cord by a thread. It was at this point in my vision that the Lord showed me that my life was CHOSEN.

As Galatians 1: 15 says, "But when He, who had set me apart, even from my mother's womb, and called me through His grace, was pleased… God (HE) had set me apart from within my mother's womb." This Scripture changed the way I looked at my life from that moment on. I now know that the devil tried to kill us both before we were born, but God had CHOSEN me before I was even formed in my mother's womb.

My Life: A Living Testimony

My middle name is Miracle, because technically, I was not supposed to survive. The way my twin sister and I were attached, even if we both were alive, the doctors would have had a difficult time with the delivery and separation.

After my sister was removed from my mother, according to Mother, the doctors could not understand why the placenta (Afterbirth) had not detached. What they did not know was that another baby was still inside, hanging on to the cord by a thread. The doctors decided to try to remove the placenta, but instead, they pulled me out by my feet. I was Alive! The only problem was my legs; my sister had lain on my legs the whole time she was dead and had hindered the circulation in my legs. The doctor suggested to my mom to have them amputated, because, I would never walk with them due to the atrophy (drying) caused by lack of circulation. Mother told the doctors, "If she survived the death of her sister; she will survive the state of her legs." My God, my God, who knew the future had a plan for me.

The Tee Shirt Experience

I slept buried under my father's arm (I will tell you later why). I used to suck my thumb and burrow my face into his underarm, feeling safe and loved. I remember one day when I was about five, my father left in the middle of the night. When I woke up, he was nowhere to be found. I asked my mother where he was, only to be told that he had gone to work in another state. I feared he would never return.

Panic now held my heart. Who would protect me now? I ran to the comfort of the bed to cry and to sniff his scent on his pillow. To my surprise, on the pillow was his tee shirt. I grabbed this great prize, bringing it close to my nose. It smelled so like him. As I breathed in his scent, I felt as if he were right there. I clung to that tee shirt for dear life, even sleeping with it until my father returned. Little did I know thirty years later that that experience would be instrumental in my introduction to my Father in heaven.

At thirty-three years old, I accepted the Lord into my life, but I did not feel His presence in my soul. I watched as other members of my church jumped and praised the Lord with songs and laughter, and here I was still feeling empty. I never wanted to show fake emotions or feelings that were not there; I was not going to be phony and pretend. As I prayed to God on my knees, with my eyes closed, I asked God to touch me in some kind of way. All of a sudden, I heard a voice telling me, "Take a deep breath through your nose." At first I was afraid, but my fears were soon allayed. As I took a deep breath through my nose, the voice asked me, "What do you smell?" I thought about it and realized it was as if I were sitting in a garden full of fragrant flowers. The deeper I inhaled, the stronger the scent became and the more at peace my heartfelt. The most wonderful feeling of peace and joy crept into my soul.

Then the voice said, "This is my scent, and just as the scent of your father's tee shirt comforted you until he returned, let My scent comfort you until I return and you will know it's Me, for I am the Lord your God, who loves you and will be there for you always." It has been 27 years since then, and I still smell His scent today. No one could have touched me in such a way but God. No one knew how the scent of my father's tee shirt affected me. Having God's scent now, I was able to transfer the love I had for my earthly father, to my heavenly father. I marveled at the love I felt for God and the love He showed me was more real now. That connection built my trust in my God in such a deep way that my faith is unmovable towards my God.

The Woman In The Tin Hut

I found time to help a woman who lived in a tin hut. She had open sores on both legs. Being unable to care for herself, much less work, she would beg passersby for food or money. I cleaned and bandaged her sores. This woman, even though she had little, always offered me some of her food. I frequently ate with her because, I knew she was lonely. I saw this woman fourteen years later. I learned that she had given birth to a daughter when she was very young and had given her to a Christian couple to raze. This couple moved away and she did not know where they left to.

This lady became very ill, and someone contacted this family. Her daughter, who had become a pediatrician, came and moved her mother where she received proper medical attention, and her legs healed.

When I went back to the old neighborhood, I assumed that she had died. To my surprise, not only was she healed, but she had a beautiful home, her daughter had built for her. I learned where she lived, and I went to visit her, thinking she would not remember me.

Fourteen years had passed since I last saw her. When she opened the door, I was taken aback by how healthy she looked. How wonderful it was to see her restored to health. She stared, and then expressed with great joy, "Don`t tell me who you are, I remember." As I looked straight into her eyes, it was as if she could see my soul. She squealed in delight and pulled me into her arms, and said "You`re that girl who came every day and cleaned my sores and kept me company." She pulled me into her house and held my hands tightly, as if she did not want to ever let go. With tears in her eyes, she brought me up to date of all that had happened after I left.

This woman told her daughter about me and she let me know how she would pray for me, asking God to bless me wherever I was. As in the past, I stayed that day for dinner. She kept thanking me for the things I had done for her, causing The Word of God to come to my remembrance, "What you do for the least of my people you do for me (Matthew 25:40)."

I was amazed to think that I had cared for an angel unaware. In gratitude, she showered me with gifts and money. I never dreamed that what I had done in my past would be reflected in my future. I thank God that I cared for others without thinking of any payment or reward. To see the happiness on her face was the greatest reward anyone could have given me.

A Visit From God

Mother became very sick and was admitted in the hospital. After thirty days, they told me that mother did not have long to live and that it was best for her to die at home. What a blow that news was to me! How would I tell my father? This burden was more than I could handle at the age of thirteen.

Once at home, I resumed my previous load of chores. My mother became very sick. She could not swallow and became weak. I kept myself busy, hoping it would take my mind off what was happening. One night I was awakened by my mother's body jerking. She could not catch her breath. I awakened my father, who was sleeping in another room. He quickly suggested I get her some water, but I was so paralyzed with worry, I could not move. He spoke to her very softly, saying, "Everything will be all right." When she calmed down, he pulled me out of the room. I noticed the look of fear in his face. I had never seen my dad look that way. He asked me to keep a close eye on my mother because he had to go and call my older siblings. My father had to walk to the police station in order to call long distance. We had no means of transportation, and the police station was about three miles away from our house. Today, I have two cars to choose from. Go figure.

While my father was gone and Mother was calm, I made my way to the kitchen to get Mother some water. Then, I started thinking about what I would do without her. I just stood there for a few minutes, and then I broke down. The thought of living without her was more than I could bear. My hands came up towards heaven and my first prayer of supplication was made, if there truly was a loving God in heaven, He would heal my mother. My eyes were closed and no sound was coming out of my mouth, but inside I was begging God to heal her. This was the first time I had ever prayed so fervently. After praying, I remained in the kitchen for a few more minutes, just to compose myself. I did not want Mother to see that I was crying. Wiping my eyes, I returned quietly and stared at mother's bed through the dimness of the early morning hour. To my astonishment my mother was sitting up and carrying on a conversation with what looked to me as a shadow of a person sitting next to her. I tried to focus my eyes better, but it seemed as if my vision was blurred. I drew closer to see who it was, but all I could see was the hazy image of a man.

Suddenly, the shadow stood up and disappeared right before my eyes. Terrified, I closed my eyes and began to scream. I screamed so loud that our neighbors ran to see what was wrong. In a fog, I heard my father's voice urging me to calm down and to tell him what had happened. He was sure that the inevitable had taken place. "Look" he said, very excited, "she is doing better than when I left." I opened my eyes very slowly. I trusted my father. My mother was sitting up and smiling at me, two things she had not done in a while. How wonderful! I told my dad about my prayer and the image of a person sitting next to Mother; he dropped to his knees and began to worship God. He determined that the image was the Lord Jesus and He had visited our home to give life to Mother. Miraculously, my mother was well enough to travel.

God Answered My Prayer

The next supplication prayer I made took place when I lived alone with my children. Again I asked God, if you are real, you will do something to change my situation." I could not cry anymore. Here I was alone with three children and no education or work experience, nothing to grasp hold of to pull us out of where we were. I decided to trust in God to do something, because I remembered all the things He had done before. I also recalled the day my Mom was so sick, and I had prayed for God to heal her, and He gave her strength to make the trip to get medical care. Yes, I believe God heard my prayer that day and deep down inside, I felt He heard this one, too.

A knock on my door woke me up. It was a young woman, asking for the lady of the house. It was a cold December day, and quickly I invited her in. She asked me if she could speak to my mother. I shyly told her I was the mother. She looked surprised due to how young I looked. I shared with her how I had no means to get around and no phone to call anyone. She told me that she worked as a case worker for this community-based center that helped with food, shelter, clothing, education, and job training. She was out in the community, looking for woman to sign up for a pilot secretarial program.

God Makes Something Out Of Nothing

The second week in January, I started classes to get my GED (General Education Diploma). The boys went to daycare where they got three meals and two snacks a day. They had other children to play with, and they were prepared for school. I honestly still could not believe all that was taking place in my life. I was actually going to school! I had always wanted to go to school. Wow! My English teacher took a liking to me. Today I call it, "The favor of God." I would stay after class to get more help with vocabulary words. two years had gone by. I had reached the eighth grade level at school. My teacher told me I was ready to take the GED test. This was my first time taking a test, and I was nervous. I did the best I could and left. The wait was on and nerve wracking. I wanted to enter the pilot class for the secretarial program so badly, but I needed the GED in order to enter.

It was the longest two weeks I had ever spent in my life. The success of my family's future depended on me doing well and with great anticipation I finally got the letter in the mail. I was scared to open it, but here we go. To my surprise, I did not pass. I needed a 225 score, and I got 223. It felt as if the ground below me fell.

Early the next morning I went straight to my English teacher. I showed her my score. I didn't even give her a chance to say anything. I just blurted out, "I'm too dumb and can't do nothing right (key number two on the seven keys was born)." She looked at me as if I were crazy and replied, "You missed it by two points. That is nothing, and now all you need to do is <u>study even harder</u>. Not to just pass, but you want to surpass. People go around this life just passing and they are Okay with that, but you must want to <u>surpass</u>." Those words hit me deeply within. She was absolutely right. I felt it all the way to my soul and key number three, "<u>What are you willing to do for your Success</u>" was born that day also.

<u>Determination</u> (key 5) became my best key to success, and three months later, I took the test again. This time I got my GED with a score of 249. I had surpassed. You could not say a thing to me. I was on my way, and no obstacle seemed too big. I stopped listening

to that voice inside that told me I would never be anything in life. <u>Key number two is to remove "the self."</u> It's that voice inside that tells you that you will never succeed at anything you desire to do. As my story unfolds, I will give you seven keys to success.

My new challenge was the secretarial program. I went into it with thoughts (key 4 <u>Visualize</u>) of success. I was going to be the best secretary I could be. I was on a roll. At my first typing class, I asked my teacher, "How fast can a person type?" She informed me that a man in the World Records typed 100 words per minute with two errors. I did not know about this World Records Book, yet I made a decision to surpass that score. The things we set out to do when we don't know better.

I asked the typing teacher if I could come after class to practice my typing. She told me I could stay as long as I wanted. I would be practicing all day. I did this for six months. Periodically, I would test myself, and my score would be 97 words per minute with four errors. This was not good. I needed to surpass the man with 100 words per minute. I had no idea that I was trying to beat a World Record. I found out later in life that this desire to surpass is what FAITH is made of. I was trying to beat something that is not normal. <u>Key number four, Visualize</u> your success. I could see myself typing over one hundred words per minute. I did not give the voice inside a chance to say a word. No one knew how much I was typing. Not even my teacher. I kept my score to myself, and less than one hundred was low for me; I did not want to fail. I just worked harder and harder trying to achieve my goal. No one told me differently. Amazing!

Beyond Real

One day, a representative from a big company came to the school looking to test three of the fastest typists for a job. My typing teacher had two students and she told me to take the test also. She felt I had practiced enough and was ready. One at a time we were ushered to a small room that had a typewriter in it with a timer that would go off when your time was up. The other two ladies went in before me, closing the door behind them to keep noise out, but I could still see because the top half was glass. I was the last to take the typing test. We all waited in the large room next to the test room. After checking our scores, the representative came into the room, and gave the job to one of the other ladies.

My heart sank, and I felt devastated. What was I thinking? I tried to walk down the hall fast. I could hear the negative voice in my head saying, "You will never succeed." The calling of my name snapped me out of it. The representative was calling me and standing next to him was my typing teacher. I thought to myself, I must have done so badly that they were going to tell me so. The representative took my hand and said, "Congratulations, you are the fastest typist we have ever seen." My typing teacher grabbed my neck and screamed, "I cannot believe it." I was now totally confused. They both had checked my scores three times to make sure they were right. I had scored 98 words per minute with two errors. My typing teacher asked me what I was trying to do. I told her what she had told me when I asked her how fast a person could type. The representative told me that he had a job with my name on it as a data entry person. My entire typing class came over to congratulate me on an outstanding score. I was not sure what to feel. I was not anticipating any of this to happen, but I tell you what, my heart had passed joy; it was in the "overwhelmed." I knew who got me there, the God I serve. Key number one is know <u>the higher power.</u>

I had surpassed the normal and had stepped into the realm of impossible, the area where God lives. What is impossible for man is possible with God. My life was turning out better than I could have imagined. The Bible said, "God uses the simple to confound the wise (I Cor 1:27, Psa 19:7)."

God Sends A Message With Me

The night before I was going to visit this church, I had a strange dream. My dreams were always dreams of evil. The devil tortured me in my dreams since I was about five years old. But, this dream was different. I was giving a message to a church. I said the same message over and over. I did not understand the message, but I was at peace as I told this congregation I had never seen before. I woke up and wrote the message down word for word on paper. I felt different as I heard the words I had never heard before. It sounded like a message of reassurance. I wrote it and went back to bed. Early that morning I called the pastor and told him the dream.

He asked if I had written it down, and I told him I did, word for word. The pastor told me to bring it with me to church, so I could read it to the congregation. I shouted, "I can't do that! This is my first time going there." I could not imagine myself doing that. For one thing, I did not know anyone there but the lady that had come to my house. Second, I did not understand the message myself. He told me that God had CHOSEN me to bring that message to the people. An outsider they will hear. He said good-bye and hung up. My stomach started turning as if a rolling pin was inside. What have I gotten myself into?

It was ten fifteen in the morning, and church service was at eleven in the morning, and here I was frozen to the corner of the bed. I did not want to go now. I had to stand in a church I had never been to and read something to them I did not know what it meant. No way! I snapped out of it when my husband tapped me on my shoulder. He was ready and excited to go to church, but not me. Why had God given me this responsibility? I had not asked for this. I was so tense that I could not bend my knees to get into the car. We got to the church. On the outside it looked small, and that made me feel a bit calmer. When we walked in and they opened the two big doors to the sanctuary, I almost fainted. It was the church in my dream, talk about "Disavow." I had been there before in my dream. It was full, and we were seated in front. Why? The praise service was really good, and I started feeling calmer as things moved on. Okay, this was not bad. The pastor started preaching on the subject of married couples who are having problems with communication. He talked on a scripture that stated, "Two cannot walk together, unless they agree" (Amos 3:3).

After the preaching was done, they acknowledged the visitors. Of course, that was us. We both stood up and stated our names. The pastor asked us if we wanted to say anything. My husband said he liked the service, and he quickly sat down. He left me standing alone. I tried to do the same as my husband, but the pastor told the congregation that I had a message from God for the church. I froze. The pastor softly told me to go ahead and read the message. As I went into my purse to get the paper, I saw all eyes were on me. As I opened the paper, my hands were shaking so hard I could not focus my eyes on the writing. As I opened the paper I felt a worm air cover my whole body. The Holy Spirit wrapped around me and calmed me down.

The Message:

For I am the Lord your God
He, who has an ear, let him hear
What the Word of God is saying
Prepare yourselves for I am coming
I hear your prayers and I will answer them
For I love you and will be with you forever.

Now, remember this was my first time going to this church. This was a brand new experience for me. I had not finished the last word, when all of a sudden people began to praise God. Than the pastor came back to the microphone and began to say, "Praise the Lord." That seemed to calm the people down. After the service was closed, the pastor pulled me into his office and explained what had happened that made the people so happy. He explained how they had been praying for ten years to hear a word from the Lord, and that He had heard our prayers. God had CHOSEN an outsider to bring the message. He said, "He knew it was of God, because I did not understand the message. They knew the message well. It was the answer they had been waiting for."

God Talks To Me In Dreams

The day I got baptized, that night I had a dream. This one scared me, because I did not understand it. It started with me standing at a doorway. I kept hearing this woman calling for help. I went to walk into the room where I heard her calling, and out of nowhere, metal bars sealed the entry to this room. I could still hear her crying for help. I became desperate because, I did not know what to do. I asked her if the devil was making her do things she did not want to do. She did not answer me; she just kept crying for help. Since I could not get to her to help her, I told her to call on God, that He was the only one who could help her. All of a sudden, I was in the room standing in front of this shadow of a woman. As my eyes came off her, I saw a horrible creature standing on the other side of the room.

It was the monster in my nightmares. It had my new Bible that was given to me at church after my baptismal in its hand. He was swinging it as if he would let it go and hit my face with it. I did not take my eyes off him. I was not afraid for some odd reason. Then the strangest thing happened. I lifted my hands and out of my mouth came the words, "In the name of Jesus Christ of Nazareth." All of a sudden I felt as if I were drifting, as if I were falling away. I tried very hard to stay in the place and get my composure. I looked to see the shadow of the woman in front of me. It was me, and I quickly turned my sight to the creature and it, too, was me. I awoke screaming.

Early that morning, I called my pastor. I told him my dream, and this was his explanation of it. "The woman that was crying for help was you in bondage. The devil had you so afraid of him that you were crying out for help. The part of the devil swinging the Bible at you, he was trying to tell you that the Bible (The Word of God) would not help you. The one that lifted her hands and called on the name of Jesus of Nazareth was the one that was renewed and had her confidence on the Lord. God delivered you from the devil's torment of fear. The drifting or feeling of falling was the Holy Spirit working in you." This was the revelation for my life. I became at peace with myself and my life. Something had happened when I came out of the water. I don't know what, but my entire attitude and feelings towards my past changed.

Experiencing God's Power through His Word

As I was gathering information about the scriptures that pertained to woman, I learned about my God. I learned about the things He had done in the past for those who obeyed Him and how He could do it today. I was so engrossed in the reading that at times I felt as if I were there watching what was going on. For example, as I was reading in Exodus, when the Red Sea split apart, the sheer thought of that experience, overwhelmed me to the point that I had to stop and catch my breath. I had been saved only six months. I was a baby-in-Christ full of get up and go. The one thing I learned very quickly was that when you want to know the truth about how to walk with God and be a true Christian, you get tried for it. The only way I found to know the Word of God so deeply to where it changed me completely, is to be tried by it and then we know it in our heart. Then and only then will it become a part of our character. In other words, we "must live" the Word of God.

The Power Of Prayer In Healing

I found my calling through dreams. Yes, it seems as if my dreams took on a different meaning in my life. They became a channel through which God spoke to me. One dream really changed my life. In this dream, I found myself driving and came up to a large tent with a banner on the front that said "Church Healing Tent." I walked in and saw that the place was full of people. They were singing a song I had never heard before, but for some reason I knew it. Six young girls were dressed in white and had tambourines in their hands. They passed in front of me singing and playing their tambourines. I waited until the last one passed, and I followed behind them to the front of the tent and took a seat. As I looked upon the stage, I saw a man scratching his legs and blood was streaming down them.

I said to myself, he needs prayer. As I thought this, something tapped me on the back of my head and said, "No, don't pray for him." I said, "Okay, I won't." Then I saw a woman on the other side of the tent jumping up and down with two tambourines in her hands. I made a sign to her to give me one. She made a gesture to come over and get one. Here came the girls again in front of me singing. I waited again for the last one to go by, and then I followed behind them singing. When I got to the entrance of the tent, there on a seat was another man. He looked very sick. I thought again to myself, he needs prayer and again, I felt the tapping on the back of my head and the voice saying, "No, don't pray for him." This time I just kept walking. As I got to where the woman was, I heard a pastor talking on the stage. I walked towards the front to hear what he was saying, and he introduced a woman whom I had never seen before. She said that she had followed all the healing tents, because she had a machine that measured the power of prayer.

Then they brought up a lady from the crowd, who was in a chair due to a disability, and they placed her in the front of the tent. The same pastor laid his hand on the lady's shoulder and his wife placed her hand on her other shoulder. All of a sudden, the pastor called me to come to pray for the lady. I was shocked, but I went to where the lady was and got down on my knees, and placed both my hands on her thigh. As soon as I rested my forehead forward on my hands to pray for her, I felt as if I were falling. I got scared. I had felt this way one time before in the dream of a woman crying for help, Then, just as fear started to set in, a soft voice said to me, "If you trust me, let yourself fall," so I stopped being afraid and I let myself go. I felt myself drifting, and a calm feeling now consumed my body. I opened my eyes and saw myself standing, looking at myself on the floor with the back of my head on the lady's leg. I saw my stomach rolling and sounds were coming out of my mouth. The lady with the machine that measured the power of prayer had put the measuring gage on my big toe, and the machine was going crazy. All of a sudden, I woke up sweating and speaking words in Spanish. Of course, I called my pastor and told him about my dream.

The one thing I could not understand was why I was looking at myself. My pastor explained to me that when a person is praying for someone who is sick, that sickness enters the person praying and the spirit of God that is in the praying person cannot be in the same body with the sickness. This is because sickness is not of God. But, when this sickness leaves the body of the person who is sick and enters the praying person, the praying person then casts off the sickness away from them both. Then the Spirit of God re-enters the praying person, and they *both are healed. This dream took the fear away from praying in* the Holy Spirit. I feel that being able to pray for the sick is a marvelous gift from God.

God Reveals My Calling And How To Use It

One year after this dream, I was in church and I got up and began walking down the outer isle by the wall. I walked by this young man who was sitting on the bench by the aisle. All of a sudden, I fell to my knees and began to cry sorrowfully for no apparent reason. I grabbed his legs and held on to them for dear life. I did not know why I was doing what I was doing, but I could not stop until as strangely as it came upon me, it left. After this incident I began to feel as if all the burdens of the world were placed on my shoulder. I could not walk into a church without falling on my face and pleading for someone. One day I became so involved that I got swollen and could not breathe. I had to go to the hospital to hear the doctors say that they could not find what was causing the swelling. My pastor came to see me in the hospital. It took him only one minute to find out what was wrong with me. His prescription was to get away. I left the hospital and went straight to a hotel in another town. There I found a hotel that was under construction and the only floors available were the 14th and 15th floors. I got a room on the 15th floor. I took a long shower and then sat in a very comfortable chair that was in front of a large bay window. I did not realize that I had been sitting there for five hours straight. I felt a strong connection to God and was listening to His voice.

In that span of time, I learned when my gift should be used and how to use it. The best thing I did was to get away. The Lord shared with me how I was to intercede only for those who could not pray for themselves. I had been taking everyone's burden and not discerning whether they were for me to pray for or if they were to pray for themselves. God revealed to me the way to tell the difference that made a whole lot of sense to me. The following time at church I was revived in faith and strength. I also found out that my heartfelt prayer for the young man kept him alive until he went to the hospital to find out that his kidneys had shut down. He got there in time to save his life.

God Gives Me A Job

I was totally committed and totally submitted to doing the work for the Lord. You could not tell me that I did not have it going on. I was so involved in the things of God, if He asked me to walk on water, I would. I now had served the Lord faithfully for five years. I was using all of the talents the Lord had given me. Now I wanted a job. I felt ready to take on a position in the Lord to work in the church wherever the need was. As the church was in meditation one snowy day, I asked the Lord for a job. This voice told me to, "*intercede*" in prayer for the children.

I understood that my place was to stand between the children and the devil. This voice explained how parents may be too involved in their own personal problems to think of the children and the devil wants to destroy them while they are young so they cannot be saved. It clarified how some adults are children in Christ, and they needed intercessory prayers also. All of a sudden I had this urge to rub my hands together. My hands became very oily. The more I tried to rub the oil off, the oilier they became. Something in my spirit told me to place my hand on the children of the church, which at the time everyone was praying and meditating with their eyes closed. It was very easy for me to touch the children without interrupting anyone. I had some adults that the Spirit had me place my hands on, too. I liked my job! I knew in my heart that I could do this job. I walked back to my seat feeling fatigued and as soon as I sat down and placed my head on my hands, I heard a voice say, "So you think you can stand between them and me? Let's see how you do when I take one of yours." I stood up and looked to see who had said that. My heart began to pound hard. I did not understand why this voice had said that. I began to wring my hands that were now dry. The oil seemed to have dried up as strangely as it appeared.

God Raised The Dead

I was so exhausted from the events that took place at church that when I got home I went straight upstairs put on my PJ.'s and went to sleep. My family was caught off guard, because I had never done anything like that before. I usually would help set up for dinner, but today was out of the usual. During this period of time, my middle son was in the streets. He was seventeen years old and had never been out in the streets before. He would come home on weekends, eat, and then leave. This particular day I had slept until 9 p.m. which was very unusual for me, and I jumped up out of my sleep with a sense of urgency. I ran down the stairs as if I had to tell my son something important. I ran up to him and told him that he could not do as he pleased in the streets.

He was prayed for and God was not going to let him do as he wanted. He had accepted the Lord in his life; therefore, God was going to stop him from doing evil." He looked at me as if I were crazy. He brushed me off and left the house. All that kept running through my mind was the Scripture that says, "God chastens those He loves (Heb 12:6)." I don't know if I read that or heard it, but it kept running through my mind. I went upstairs and began to get dressed. My husband asked me what I was doing, I told him that we were going somewhere. Not even an hour later there was a knock on our door. It was my nephew, he was hysterical. Once he calmed down, he told me he had seen an ambulance taking my son to the hospital. I looked at my husband who looked at me as if I had had some kind of insight. When we got to the hospital, I found out that my son had been hit on the head with a bat and a metal pipe several times. Apparently, a gang was waiting for him, and three of them had jumped him and beat him until they thought he was dead. The owner of the store across the street saw them beat my son, and he called the police. My son was pronounced dead at the cine.

He was put on a respirator and was going into surgery to stop the bleeding in his brain. This was not done to save his life, but to clean him up. The doctors had given him up for dead. I was left alone for a few minutes with my son before they were going to take him to surgery. He looked pale and was cold. I asked God if He was calling my son to his sleep or is the devil trying to destroy him. I told God, "I would give my son only to Him." Then, it came to my remembrance, what that voice had said to me, "Let's see how you do when I take one of yours." I told God, "I will fight the devil tooth and nail; I will not allow the devil to destroy my son." Like the mist of a cool wind, a comforting voice filled my soul and I felt warm and at peace. The voice said, "If you have faith in Me the size of a mustard seed, I WILL raise your son on the third day." I knew just what I had to do. I had listened to my pastor talk about the power of faith and how God can increase our faith when we ask Him. I knew that if I did not walk this walk with faith, my son would not live. Just then the hospital staff came in and wheeled my son into surgery. As they were taking him away, I knew in my heart God would not let him die as long as I had faith in Him.

It was around three in the morning when they took my son to surgery. Exhausted, I asked my husband to take me home. By this time my whole family knew what had happened and was there in the waiting room. My pastor showed up and half of the congregation. I knew that in order to keep the faith, I needed to stay away from people with less faith. The only way I could do that was to avoid everyone. I apologized for leaving and went home to get some rest. I slept only for a few hours, but it felt as if I had slept for eight hours straight. I believe my earlier nap had something to do with it. I got up at seven thirty in the morning and went to the hospital. I arrived at eight thirty in the morning and just as I got there, my son was coming out of surgery. The doctor that did the surgery came to me and explained the procedure that had taken place. He explained that he had opened my son's skull, stopped the bleeding, placed a jelly-like bag in his head to prevent the brain from shifting around, and put metal clamps in to hold the skull back together. The doctor had me sign a paper before he had done the surgery, asking that if my son's heart stopped during the surgery, that he would not be resuscitated. In addition, if by eleven in the morning on the third day he showed no signs of brain activity, he would be disconnected from the respirator and pronounced dead.

My son survived the surgery and was in the critical care unit. They allowed only the parents in to see him for only two minutes. The doctor explained to us how he was going to look and how the room was set up with lots of machines. My son had three nurses on a shift of 24 hours. One was a praying nurse and she watched him at night; this was of

God. I now knew that God was in the midst of things. Feeling confident that my son was in good hands, I went home. My family got mad, because I did not stay in the hospital next to my son. They could not believe that I would leave my son in the hospital in such critical condition. To them he could die at any minute, to the doctors he was already dead, but to me he was blessed. To me, he was alive and in God's hands.

I did not feel that I needed to be there. All I would be doing was waiting for him to be pronounced dead, and I was not going to allow anything or anyone to deter my faith from what God had told me. I was called every two hours on my son's status; therefore; I did not need to sit at the hospital and wait. Wait for what? I did not go back to the hospital after my son came out of surgery. My husband would go and stay almost all day while I stayed home cooking and cleaning as usual. I slept well and was in no way worried about my son. This made no sense to everyone at the hospital. They felt that this was my way of dealing with what was going on. Little did they know that my trust was totally in God! No wavering. I had total confidence in God's power. Three days went by very fast. I thanked God for the speed. If it would have gone by slowly, I don't know if I could have lasted. At 11:15 a.m. on the third day, I got a call from the nurse that took care of my son at night; she stayed to see him taken off the machines, she was crying hysterically.

The first words that might come out of your mouth, hearing her crying like that and knowing what was going on at that time, would be "What is wrong?" Right? Well, out of my mouth came the words, "Give me the good news." That faith was so strong in me that no negative words could come out. She stopped crying and asked me if someone had told me. I asked her, told me what? She said, "The doctors, the lawyers, the coroner and the family were here to witness your son taken off the respirator and pronounced dead. The doctors waited 15 minutes before pronouncing him dead, when all of a sudden he woke up and grabbed the hand of the doctor who was taking out the last tube. He was awake and asking for his mother." I don't know where the phone ended up, but I was out the door and heading for the hospital. All I could do was cry for joy. God had done what He had said He was going to do. He raised my son from the dead. FAITH! I knew it now, not just in my mind but in my soul. I don't know how I got to the hospital, but when I walked into the room my son saw me and with his hand he let me know he was alive and wanted me to get to his side.

My son recovered completely, and the doctors were totally astounded at his recovery. This was a young man they had pronounced dead. They could not explain how he survived.

My God's work did not stop there. When God does anything, He does it all the way. I don't know if this is correct English, but you know what I mean. While recovering, he somehow would get out of his bed and wander into other patients' rooms and would be praying or telling them to wake up that God had woke him up.

My son believed God could do it for them also. My son was sent home two weeks after his incident. He was weak and not walking well, but he was alive. As far as I was concerned, God kept His promise to raise my son from the dead on the third day, if I had faith in Him and God did what He said He would do. He is a Promise Keeper.

My son's right side was still paralyzed. The doctors told us that he might never recover completely. He had an appointment two weeks after they sent him home to see how he was doing. I went with my son to this appointment. They did a CAT scan and a neurologist checked him. The neurologist said he had 100% full function of his body. He could not explain how, but he told my son that God was giving him another chance at life and he should not waste it. My son then had to go see the surgeon that did the operation on his head. He needed the CAT scan pictures before he saw my son. We went to his office and the surgeon came in. He looked at my son and asked if he was a twin.

My son asked him why. The surgeon told us that the CAT scan pictures were not his and he sent my son to get another CAT scan done. This time he went down with him. The CAT scan did not show the jelly bag that he had put in my son's head, and there were no metal clamps, which he had put in to keep his scull together. The doctor did not even find a hair line fracture on his scull that would show that he had had an operation. It was as if my son had never been in the hospital at all. He could not explain what he was looking at. He came out of the room and held my son's hand. He said, "Either you are not the same young man I did surgery on, or there is a God." The neurologist told him the same thing. He got a clean bill of health. The only evidence that he had had surgery was the scar on his head, and his hair had grown so fast that even it was covered.

Throughout all that had happened I was still calm. It had not hit me what God had done. We were walking out of the hospital and towards the parking lot to the car. It had snowed the day before about eleven inches of snow. I was walking ahead of my son trying to hurry to get to the car. As I was walking in the snow, a voice said to me, "Turn around and see the glory of God." I turned around and saw my son walking towards me. It looked as if he were walking on air. His appearance looked different, as if he were brand new.

That was when it hit me. My son, who was dead, was not only alive, but was also walking and in his right mind. I fell to my knees in the snow: my whole body was shaking at the greatness of God. I could not stand. I could see the power of God all around my son. I knew that only God could do what my eyes were seeing.

You Don't Know The God I Serve

I got up one morning and decided to go to the local college. I went to the admissions office and asked for information on how to become a student there. I filled the application out and was told to make an appointment with one of the admissions officers, so I did. To my surprise, the admissions officer assigned to me was someone I had met when I was doing my GED. I was there early for my appointment. I like to make a good impression. In the meeting he looked over my application. He asked me if I had gone to some other school for training or vocational type of school. I told him that the only schooling I had was done while I was preparing for my GED.

He said, "You cannot attend college! You have no previous education." He told me I would have to take college preparation classes before I could be considered for college. He told me to come back and see him when I had taken the classes. I left his office with a knot in my throat. I could not walk home fast enough. I did not want to break down in the middle of the street. As my door closed behind me, I fell to the floor. I cried out to my Lord, "talk to me, and tell me what to do." A soft voice said, "Get up." I knew it was an order. God was speaking directly to me. My crying stopped, and I was standing and listening. The voice told me, to go back to that man and "Tell him to test you first before he makes a judgment call. That he did not know the God you served." I began to shout with joy. My God would make a way out of no way.

I knew him in the power to raise the dead, now I was going to know him in the power to move mountains. I washed my face and fixed myself up. I walked back to the college with power in my soul. God told me that, "I could do all things through Christ who strengthens me (Phil 4:14)." I believe what He said to me. I walked up to the receptionist and asked her if I could please see the same admission officer; It was urgent. She called his office and told him that I needed to see him urgently. He told her to send me in. I walked into his office, and before he could say a word, I told him to give me a test first before he judged my ability to do college. He looked puzzled. I guess he had never had a person run up to him as I did. Then he called the receptionist into his office and told her to set me up to take the entrance exam. I turned around and walked behind her without saying a word to him. I had never felt as confident in myself as I did that day. I could not believe I was talking to him with such power.

God Takes The Simple To Confound The Wise

Test day came fast. I had prayed and asked God to help me, if it was His will for me to go to college. I had never taken a test before, except for my GED. The lady that was giving out the tests told me that I had to take five different sections, and I had one hour. What she did not say was that each test had one hour. I picked up the first one and sat down. I could not understand one word on this test. I started to panic, but, this voice came to me and said, "Fear not, for I will not fail you nor forsake you (Josh 1:5)" I became so relaxed that I did not feel as if I was taking a test. To my surprise, I knew what I was doing, and before I knew it, I had done all five sections in forty-five minutes. Can you believe this? I was so focused on what I had to do that I didn't even notice the time. The things we do when we don't know any better. When I turned in the last section, the lady told me that I was done. I looked at her surprise. I was not aware that I was whizzing through these tests. I waited for them to score all five sections. It was done fast.

Before I knew it, she handed me my scores and congratulated me on a job well done. When I looked at them, it seemed as if they were all low; 49, 55, 48, 52, 52. I asked her to explain them to me. She told me that the highest scores for each test were 55 points, and I had almost made all the highest scores. She pointed out that I had passed all five sections (let me write it big) ABOVE AVERAGE. You could not tell me that there is no God. He didn't just help me past the test, He made me surpass. This is the God I serve. I took my test scores and went right to the admission officer's office and showed him my test scores. I said, "Read them and then tell me if I can or cannot do college." His eyes opened up so wide. He said, "With these scores, you can take all regular classes." He signed my admission papers, and I was off and running. Nothing could stand in my way. Right?

Wisdom And Power At God's Hand

I went to register for classes, but I needed an advisor to advise me of the classes I was to take. I was appointed an advisor, who by God's doing, was a Christian woman. She was so nice and encouraging; God holds the present and the future. He knows what is ahead and sets up accordingly. What would have been the chances of not only scoring above average, but also having a saved advisor? You tell me! She set me up with twenty-four (6 classes) credits my first semester. I asked her to let me take that amount. I knew that I could do them all. She trusted my wishes and prayed with me about it. This is when _The Seven Keys To Success_ came into play.

God blessed me with a chance to present these keys at a workshop for my church members and invited guests. A tape of that workshop was made and is available where this book is sold. This tape is anointed and power-inducing. In order for God's Word to become a part of your character, you must be tried by it, and then and only then shall it be written in the tablet of your heart, where it will bear fruit. It is my belief that when you have gone through and have learned how to get through, that you must share it with others, so that they may learn to go through with victory. Then they, in return, share it with others so that others will learn also. It's the Gospel of Jesus Christ that is shared. What he has done for us and can do for everyone that calls upon His name.

Know what you would like to happen in your life and see if it fits into God's plan for your life. Anything that has positive growth of any kind for your life is in God's plan. In 3 John 1:2, it states God's hope for us. "To prosper and be in good health as our Spirit prospers." There is nothing I could say to clarify that statement. You must want what God wants in order to be blessed beyond anything you can imagine for yourself. Start with the End in mind.

The Master Teacher- Teaches Me
How To Study Smart Not Hard

You know when God is trying to bless you, when the devil fights you hard. I started my first semester in college. I can't believe I said that. My greatest dream was coming true. I set myself up to succeed. I had all my books and class syllabuses. But, I had no idea where to start. I felt overwhelmed. I got down on my knees and asked God to help me. I found out that God is not moved by tears. He is moved by you recalling His promises and letting Him know that you know them and you are willing to stand on them. This is where my deliverance scripture came in again. "I can do all things through Christ who strengthens me (Phil 4:13)." I had not taken any college prep courses and I had no instructions on planning the course of action. I did not know where to start. I felt drained and I had not even started school. The night before classes were to start, I really felt overwhelmed. I was so exhausted from trying to figure where to start that I went to sleep. At three o'clock in the morning I woke up feeling sure of what to do. The Lord put on my heart to open His Word and read. I almost said "no" because I had to get ready to start school, and I needed time to get ready. But, the Holy Spirit said to trust in the Lord.

I thought to myself, He has brought me out of worse jams, so I will trust Him on this one. I read until six in the morning. Then I got up and went to bed and slept until nine in the morning. My first class did not start until eleven in the morning. All of a sudden, I knew what to do. I put all my syllabuses in order and wrote what chapters had to be read, and I had my notebooks in order. I began to read a chapter in all my books and it was as if it was not me. The Lord was teaching me _how to study smart, not hard_. The Lord taught me how to do college by reading His Word first. Then He told me to take every heading and turn them into a question. He told me to do this before reading each paragraph. Then find the answer and write it down as your notes. The Holy Spirit shared with me how

32

each paragraph has one idea and the writer must give the definition to the idea. Example; Short term memory (topic = idea) definition= A memory that last only 20 seconds. The question would look like this: What is short term memory? I did this to every paragraph in each chapter and write the answers down. I would study my answers before a test and I would get 100 on them.

The Seven Keys to Success

Key # 1.   *Remove Self* - the Voice inside that talks NEGATIVE from what God's Word tells us that we are and can be.

Key # 2.   *Know Your Higher POWER* That Only God Can Do All GREAT Things in Your Life, and you know it, and you give him all the Glory.

Key # 3.   Are you *Willing* To Do Whatever It Takes To Obtain SUCCESS? Let nothing hold you back even if you must suffer or be in pain? God tells us that <u>IF</u> you be Willing, He will supply the Power.

Key # 4.   *VISUALIZE Yourself* How or Where You Want To Be. Chose how you want to look and feel. We must work towards achieving it. Have a purpose for doing it.

Key # 5.   *DETERMINE* To Succeed At All You Do. Do It As If you're doing it For the Glory of God.

Key # 6   *PERSISTANCE* Let Nothing Stop You From Obtaining Your Success. No Illness, No Financial Problems, No Personal Problems, and Most of all, yourself.

Key # 7.   *COMMITMENT* This is The Most Grounded Key. You Must Be Committed To Serve The Lord, No Matter What. This Key Seals All The Other Keys. This Key Makes You Show That God Is In Your Life By the way you stand firm on your commitments and follow through with what you started no matter what obstacles stand in your way of holding on to your commitment.

God blessed me with a chance to present these keys at a workshop for my church members and invited guests. It is my belief that when you have gone through and have learned how to get through, that you must share it with others, so that they may learn to go through with victory. Then they, in return, share it with others so that others will learn also. It's the Gospel of Jesus Christ that is shared. What he has done for us and can do for everyone that calls upon His name.

<u>Know</u> what you would like to happen in your life and see if it fits into God's plan for your life. Anything that has positive growth of any kind for your life is in God's plan. In 3 John 1:2, it states God's hope for us. "To prosper and be in good health as our Spirit prospers." There is nothing I could say to clarify that statement. You must want what God wants for you in order to be blessed beyond anything you can imagine for yourself. Start with the End in mind.

Nothing To Small For God

Due to an illness I could not do my new job and because I had less than a year, I did not qualify for disability. I did not have any kind of money, not even for a piece of gum. Here I was, between a rock and a hard place. My grandson, who was staying with me that weekend, wanted a ham burger and fries. I went into my prayer mode. I know my God can do anything. I had ten dollars in the bank, and if I took that out, my account would be closed. We were leaving to walk to the bank to get the ten dollars and go get him what he wanted. As we stepped into the hallway, the mailman stopped me and gave me an envelope. It looked like a government check inside. I went back inside and opened it. It was a Social Security check for eight thousand dollars. I called my pastor, because I did not know where it had come from. He asked me if the name was correct and the address. I said "Yes." He said, "Then it's yours." I forgot that four years ago I got ill and had to stop working for almost a year. I had applied and was denied. You know it was God. He is on time always. It may not be on your time, but on time nevertheless. I looked at my grandson, who had no idea what was going on. I told him the good news and he may not have understood, but he was happy, and I was ecstatic. My God, my God.

Healing From The Past

I started getting small strokes. One morning I could not get up. I had suffered a big stroke. Now, I was in big trouble. The stress of the stroke made my eyes burst in the back and caused me to be blind. One night I prayed as hard as I could. I could not understand why I was not healed. I had so many people praying for me, but nothing happened. Three years and I was no better. I was told that I would not walk nor see again. These people did not know the God that I served. I saw him raise the dead. Whose report was I going to believe? After three years in a bed of affliction, it hit me. All that reading I did before the stroke, I fed off that reading for three years. Do you hear what I am saying? So, I searched God's Word that had been written in the tablets of my heart. I know this sounds so cliché, but it is true. I remembered all the stories in the Bible that had healing in them.

I recalled the people who were healed and saw in my mind how they got healed. When I got to the woman with the issue of blood, I heard the Lord say, "Touch me the way she did and you will be made whole." Now, I searched on the difference of her touch from the others that were touching Him. I figured it out, and I did it. The next thing I knew I was in my bathroom brushing my teeth. My nurse came to feed me my can of Ensure and was so shocked that she had to sit on my empty bed. How do you tell someone that you touched God and were healed? She had seen me just the day before. It made a believer out of her.

The Miracle And Healing Power of God

I got bit by a Brown Recluse Spider on the right side of my back. This is a deadly spider and I was in bad shape. It started off looking like a target, a small circle with a white dot in the middle. I asked my husband to see what was on my back, and he said I had a pimple. It hurt, but not too badly. In three days it went from the size of a quarter to the size of a dinner plate. And two more weeks later I woke up with a hump three inches high on my back. I went to the Emergency Room and was admitted to the hospital pending a biopsy of the hump. The results came back a Brown Recluse Spider Bite, but nothing was found in the hump. I was sent home with pain medication.

The mother of the church came to see me. She suggested that I get into a tub of hot water and Epson Salt. I was in so much pain, what did I have to lose? As soon as my back hit the water, I felt relieved. I asked my husband to dry my back, and he shouted that stuff was coming out of the biopsy hole. Back to Emergency we went.

When the doctor pulled the towels (plural) away, he jumped back asking what that was on my back. I said, "That's my spider bite." I was rushed into surgery. The bacteria had eaten a hole in my back that the surgeon said he could fit both his fists into it. A week later I was sent home with nurses coming to pack and unpack the hole three times a day. This went on for almost a year and twenty different antibiotics. With no cure in sight, a surgeon was brought in on my case. She suggested removing all the area infected and have skin draft placed over the area. She introduced me to her surgical team, and a date was set. I went to the hospital for pre-op testing the day before. I was put into a room for the surgeon to mark my back for the surgery in the morning. She had explained how she would have to remove three and a half inches above the infected area. The two nurses that would be working with the surgeon removed my bandages and the four and a half feet of gauze my nurse had placed in the hole that morning. One minute later the surgeons walked in to measure and mark my back. Now, remember the two nurses who had removed my bandages? They were standing in front of me, waiting on the surgeon to mark me.

All of a sudden, it felt painful what she was doing. She stopped and walked in front of me and took my hands in hers. I wondered what was going on. She had tears forming in her eyes. She said, "I prayed that you would not have to have this surgery. With your diabetes, you would not heal and you would be deformed." The outcome was not good. As she squeezed my hands, she uttered, "You don't need the surgery. The hole is gone. You are healed." My God, my God!

The two nurses looked confused. They both had to see what the surgeon was talking about. The bandages' were sitting on the bed next to me. They knew a hole had been there a second ago. They touched the spot where a hole was and found nothing there. Nothing but God could have done this miracle. If those nurses were unbelievers, they became believers now, and if the surgeon did not believe in prayers, I know she does now. You have never seen anyone so happy and grateful to God for healing me as my husband.

The Good Fight Of Faith (Breast Cancer)

All was well. My husband and I were preaching at this church and I started a tape ministry for members who could not make it to church. My sermons had my testimonies in them. God had done so much in my life that gave me many sermons to talk about. I knew Evangelism was my calling. When you believe in something and you know it's true and real, you want everyone to have it. That is the reason I state that, *"My Life Is A Living Testimony."* I would not have CHOSEN to obtain all these experiences, so that I could preach about them, as I said, "The life of the chosen is not a life of chance, but a life of precision." Two years after my healing of the spider bite, I came down with breast cancer. I was taking a shower and shaving under my arms, when my pinkie rubbed a small ball on my left breast. Not sure if I was feeling something there, I asked my husband to feel it. He felt the small ball under my skin. Here we go again.

I paid it no mind. My breast was large and I had lumps all over both of them. In two weeks the lump had grown into the size of a calf ball. Now I was worried. I went to see my OB/GYN (Obstetrics and Gynecology), who referred me to the breast center for a mammography (X-ray). I had a biopsy done on the lump that was now the size of an orange. I had this done on a Monday and Wednesday at seven in the afternoon, the call came in. I placed the call on speaker phone so my husband and sister could hear the results. My right breast was fine, but my left had two kinds of cancer. The doctor referred me to a surgeon, who referred me to a plastic surgeon that worked with her to do the reconstruction. Instead of being afraid, I was excited. I w as going to get a body make-over. What the devil meant for my bad, God turned it into a blessing. Surgery day came fast. Remember, I was a forty D size bra. When the plastic surgeon came to see me for surgery, I told him I wanted small and perkier breasts. He laughed, and I went under. The next thing I remember was waking up in ICU (Intensive Care Unit). My first instinct was to wait for the pain. I asked

God to please keep me from too much pain. I could not deal with pain. The next day I was moved to a regular room.

All of a sudden, I felt this urge to get up and walk. I called the nurse and told her "my desire to get out of bed." She said "That I would need some pain medication first," but, I said "No." I wanted to get out of bed and walk. She came back with three other nurses and a walker. I could hear my Lord telling me not to fear the pain. All four lifted me up and put me on my feet. I grabbed a hold of the walker, and off I went. I walked the entire hallway and back to my room, still no pain. Five days later I was sent home. No pain. Three weeks later, no pain. It was too good to be true. It's been seven years, and I'm still waiting for the pain. I felt very good. I would peek under my bandages to see if I could see my new breast. I was excited to see my new body. The bandages came off, and I loved my new breast. The plastic surgeon had done a wonderful job, small and perkie.

God Reminds Me Of What Is To Come
(A New Heavenly Body)

The joy of my new body was short lived. I believe God gives us His strength to endure the things of this world. While we are alive in this world we will suffer many things, but thank God for giving us an Armor to wear to be able to STAND against the whales of the devil. As you would know, three days after the bandages came off, my wounds opened up. The one in my stomach felt like a broken zipper opening up. Both incisions on my breast opened up. I had to get all the dead skin removed from all my incisions. What happened? I felt no pain. Now I had nurses coming three times a day to pack me with medicated gauze and unpack me. Here we go again, like the spider bite. Lord, have mercy on me was my constant prayer. What had I done to have this happen to me? Don't ask this question, if you don't want the answer.

One morning I was taking a shower. I had taken the bandages off to wash the wounds with antibacterial soap as I was told to do by the nurses. Half of the wall facing the shower was a mirror. I had not looked at my wounds. I took my shower before the nurse would come to put new bandages on. As I stepped out of the shower I looked up and was horrified at what I saw. The hole in my stomach was the worst. I began to panic and cry out to God, "How are these holes on my body going to close?" I knew there was no way for them to close. The gaps were too wide and deep. Then, I heard a still small voice say, "Why do you fret about the look of your body, when it cannot enter in heaven (I Cor 15:50-53). I will give you a new body, one that will never get sick, get cancer, or have diabetes." I felt as if someone had slapped the back of my head and said "get a grip." I came out of that bathroom with a new perspective in my life. My goal now was to make it to heaven and get that new body. The Bible tells us that, "No flesh or blood will enter into heaven." "Yes," we are to take care of the body we have, which should be the temple of God, but it is good to know that a better one awaits you.

My wounds have closed up almost to the point of small scars. I thank God for all the opportunities He gives me to learn the truth of His power and will for me. These lessons are extreme, but the lesson is learned deep down into my heart and soul and mind. I rejoice in my healing, and I praise God for loving me so much that He sent His only son (John 3:16) to pay the price for my Salvation and for Eternal life.

Now share my lessons learned to others. Because I know firsthand many challenges that many will face in their life, I can tell them how my God delivered me. I have many stories of challenges that I faced in my life, but the book would have been too large to carry. I selected the ones I felt edified God the most. I pray that as you read this book you find that your challenges are smaller or larger compare to mine and you too can overcome them with God's help. Give him your <u>Un-Chosen Life</u>, and let Him lead you. You will find that your life with Christ Jesus is the best life you ever had. I know, I have lived the life He <u>chose</u> for me. Praise the Lord always.